Peter Brook

Peter Brook is one of the world's best-known theatre directors. Outstanding in a career full of remarkable achievements are his productions of *Titus Andronicus* (1955) with Laurence Olivier, *King Lear* (1962) with Paul Scofield, and *The Marat/Sade* (1964) and *A Midsummer Night's Dream* (1970), both for the Royal Shakespeare Company. Since moving to Paris and establishing the International Centre for Theatre Research in 1970 and the International Centre for Theatre Creation when he opened the Bouffes du Nord in 1974, he has produced a series of events which push at the boundaries of theatre, such as *Conference of the Birds* (1976), *The Ik* (1975), *The Mahabharata* (1985) and *The Tragedy of Carmen* (1981) to name but a few. His films include *Lord of the Flies* (1963), *King Lear* (1970), *The Mahabharata* (1989) *Tell Me Lies* (restored 2013) and *Meetings with Remarkable Men* (restored 2017). His hugely influential books, from *The Empty Space* (1968) to *The Quality of Mercy* (2013), have been published in many languages throughout the world.

Peter Brook

TIP OF THE TONGUE

Reflections on Language and Meaning

NICK HERN BOOKS
London
www.nickhernbooks.co.uk

A NICK HERN BOOK

Tip of the Tongue
first published in Great Britain in 2017
by Nick Hern Books Limited,
The Glasshouse, 49a Goldhawk Road, London W12 8QP

'Skyscraper' is based on a speech given at the British
Library in June 2016.

'When is a Space Not a Space?' and 'The Mirror' are
based on speeches written for Blanche Marvin's Empty
Space Awards.

Front cover image: *The Tower of Babel* by Pieter Bruegel
the Elder (Hulton Fine Art Collection/Getty Images)
Author photo by Régis d'Andeville

Designed and typeset by Nick Hern Books
Printed in the UK by CPI Group (UK) Ltd

A CIP catalogue record for this book is available from
the British Library

ISBN 978 1 84842 672 6

To all those who over the years have stimulated the questioning and the experiences I describe.

This cannot be dedicated to one person—to you all with gratitude.

Contents

Prologue

A long time ago when I was very young, a voice hidden deep within me whispered, 'Don't take anything for granted. Go and see for yourself.' This little nagging murmur has led me to so many journeys, so many explorations, trying to live together multiple lives, from the sublime to the ridiculous. Always the need has been to stay in the concrete, the practical, the everyday, so as to find hints of the invisible through the visible. The infinite levels in Shakespeare, for instance, make his works a skyscraper.

But what are levels, what is quality? What is shallow, what is deep? What changes, what always stays still?

This can now lead us together through many forms, at many times, in many places. To begin with, what is a word?

If we say to a child, 'Be good', the word 'good' has its everyday commonplace meaning. If we rise above the ground level, the word 'good' brings us to finer and finer shades of goodness. Even more so in French—'*Soyez sage*', the parents say to their children, using '*sage*', a word for wisdom. There are so many words that contain such promises. A 'divine' evening. 'Divine' belongs to the sky. To use 'divine' casually makes the 'sacred' lose all its meaning.

In the pages that follow, we will explore together the sometimes comic and often subtle differences between two languages that have lived together for so long—French and English.

With William the Conqueror, the Latin-based language penetrated into English and vastly enriched its vocabulary. For us, the

Norman invasion was a blessing. On the other hand, the Anglo-Saxon idiom seemingly never penetrated beyond Agincourt. Thanks to this, French, with a much smaller vocabulary, became a vehicle for pure and crystal-clear thought. I must, however, warn the reader that all comments on the French language in this book come necessarily from an Anglo-Saxon point of view.

After nearly half a century of living in France, when I ask for something, clearly, in a shop, the person serving me winces and immediately answers me in English. Either it is fear of not understanding the foreigner or else the pain of hearing their fine language mangled, its precise rules ignored. This has been a starting point for relishing the difference between two languages which are like chalk and cheese.

Over the years, I have wondered what is the mysterious relationship between a word and its real meaning. Words are often a necessity.

Words, like chairs and tables, are necessary tools for navigating the everyday world. But it is all too easy to let the word itself take first place. The essence is meaning. Silence already has a meaning, meaning that is searching to be recognised through a world of changing forms and sounds.

Our lazy habit is to generalise. We will discover that, much as the atom—once opened—contains a universe, in the same way if we linger fondly within a phrase, we find within each word and every syllable that the resonances are never twice the same.

PART ONE

Words Words Words

When the very first pre-Neanderthal man slammed two stones together, scraped them to make a sharp edge that could cut, he made a grunt. Centuries went by as he painfully developed his tools, and at the same time he developed his grunts and growls into early forms of speech.

He needed to communicate his strivings to another human creature. Amongst the first fragments of meaning came syllables that corresponded to 'good' and 'no good'. As he discovered that there were many steps in between these two, they became targets, and the way towards them became 'better' or 'worse'. Time crept by, and the sense of a goal, and of the long distance to be travelled to approach them, made 'better' or 'worse' an instant encouragement to continue or a source of anger or despair. Better or worse became all that was needed for activity to continue.

Then for a million reasons, religion appeared, and at once the great unattainable became 'good' and 'bad'. God became the unattainable, bad became 'evil'. From 'evil' it was a short and ever-so-useful step to the Devil. And so evil became incarnated into demons and good into angels leading to God.

From this came the greatest of human discoveries, that at every moment in every manifestation, every form, every action, 'better' or 'worse' were the great motors of evolution and transformation.

Then it became clear that there are levels for everything. For the artisan, for the artist, for the contemplative. At any moment there is a possibility of 'better' and an inevitable giving-way—gradually mankind became aware of levels—something expressed by a ladder with angels helping man up and devils making him slip and dragging him down.

Today, the image that presents itself is the skyscraper. Sometimes the elevators work, but at other times (as during and after a tornado) one must climb on foot. The effort is enormous, more and more painful, and for each one of us there is a time when no more effort is possible. One looks at the number of the floor one has reached and realises how tiny it is compared with the number of floors to be climbed before one emerges on to the open gallery at the top, with its vision of the sky and its brilliant light. And from every floor the view changes—for the better: the field of vision is wider and wider. More can be seen and understood. Better to be high up, worse to be in the dark dampness of the basement.

Now we see that in every activity in life a sense of levels is present in us. We need to go

no further than a single word. And within it,
an endless scale of finer or coarser vibration,
of finer or coarser meanings.

Tip of the Tongue

'Je ne comprends pas ce qu'il dit. Pas un mot.' (I can't understand a word he says.) This reaction from someone in the audience at the first preview of our first production in Paris with our international group of actors left me speechless.

The actor had come to us from the Royal Shakespeare Company with perfectly trained projection and diction. I stood at the back of the stalls and could follow every syllable. If I could understand, why couldn't the French? It took me a long time to discover the solution to this enigma.

Where did it all begin? With the creation in Paris in 1970 of the International Centre for Theatre Research. Three years had gone by for a group made of actors from many parts of the world, three years of exploring sounds with our tongues, our throats and our chests. Our own languages had been put aside, or rather had served as fascinating elements of exchange—Japanese against Bambara, English into Portuguese, Farsi or Armenian. We had gone back to the earliest languages—Avesta, Ancient Greek—and the adventurous poet Ted Hughes had written for us a new language of his own, Orghast, in which the meaning of a word was uniquely carried by its shape and sound. We never worked in a theatre, always playing in fresh, unexpected situations, from supermarkets to ancient ruins and African villages.

We returned to Paris to reopen a forgotten theatre, the Bouffes du Nord, and this time all the words came from Shakespeare. We were preparing to play *Timon of Athens* in French. It was here that the fundamental difference between French and English suddenly became painfully clear. A French group was joining us for the first time, and our actors were fascinated. For our group, it was a new experience to be with the French performers, and everyone welcomed the chance of being shaken out of their usual habits.

The challenge, too, was fascinating. On that first morning of rehearsals there was an interesting mixture sitting in a circle on the floor, ready to work. All went smoothly, the two groups liked and appreciated one another.

At the outset of our International Centre for Theatre Research, I asked my invaluable co-director, Micheline Rozan, 'Where can I find a writer to work with us who doesn't wish to impose his own vision? Shakespeare never did, but who today?' She answered, 'You must meet Jean-Claude Carrière.'

When I met Jean-Claude, there was an immediate friendship and understanding. All his experience had been in film, writing scenarios with directors such as Buñuel, so he knew that a writer must be part of a team. I invited him to our international group to watch exercises and improvisations. Soon he was taking part in them. For *Timon*, I asked him to make a new French text.

In all his writing, Jean-Claude looked for clarity and reacted against the acrobatics of the Shakespeare translators who tied the language into knots in their attempts to preserve the complexities of the original. This comes from a deeply rooted idea that 'poetic' means a 'flowery' language, halfway to singing. Shakespeare's greatest lines are simple and flow naturally. Jean-Claude tried to find a way of being true to the purity and limpidity of the best French poets, whose language is never poetic in a self-conscious attempt to be literary. So he peppered his text with words that easily carried the thought and yet were transparent: *'rayonnants'* (radiant), he called them. It was then up to the actor by his moment-to-moment presence to add the dimension—the rhythm and the music of a phrase—that is inevitably lost in translation.

When we began to work in our new space, I often had to stop the French actors. 'You are playing too fast,' I would tell them. 'In Shakespeare, it's not just the idea that drives you, it is the fine overtones that need time to vibrate through each word. Don't hurry! Listen how the English actor breaks up every line.' The French actors began to speak more slowly, and this was our undoing.

I had failed to recognise that, if in English we speak words, the French speak thoughts. A thought is an instantaneous flash that is too fast for our usual means of perception. A thought is complete—if it's broken, it loses its meaning. This is why French is so quick, so nimble, so light—the expression of a rapier-sharp intelligence. A thought is a whole. Following the rules of French grammar, each sentence has to be conceived complete before it is uttered. The questions of gender, masculine or feminine, of verbs, singular or plural, are already resolved, and the phrase is spoken with the precision of a mathematical formula. There is no improvising on the way.

We can experience this very simply. Take any proverb that comes to mind. A proverb is ready-made; it is inscribed in us from childhood as one complete thought. 'Many hands make light work.' 'Too many cooks spoil the broth.' 'A stitch in time saves nine.' If we break the line into—a stitch, *pause*, in, *pause*, time—it becomes so awkward that it no longer makes sense.

The French are trained to know the end of any sentence before they start it, even the end of a complete paragraph. A cultivated speaker can have what he has spoken transcribed and printed with no need for corrections. In normal spoken English, it is natural to hum and haw from the very first word, as we feel our way towards what we want to say. However, were the same words and the same imagery part of an actor's task in a play of Shakespeare's such as *Love's Labour's Lost* or *Twelfth Night*, the exact opposite would be true. An actor must not hum and haw, but he must always, at each performance, return to the state of not knowing what comes next. Then the most well-worn words like 'To be or not to be' are each time reborn.

In French, the melody passes through the vowels while in English the propeller is the consonant. English has a wide range of tones that arise naturally. On the other hand, French is almost all on one note: this does not make for monotony—it has its own very subtle music.

Hold a sheet of tissue paper in front of the mouth. Now say, 'p ... t ...' in a French sentence—for example, '*Il faut partir*'—and the paper will hardly move. The sound is 'Il ... au arir', with an almost inaudible 'p', but they will instinctively know what the sentence is. Say firmly in English 'PuT it on ToP', and the paper will quiver. This is the secret.

An even more vivid example of the percussive nature of consonants is in a line from Shakespeare's sonnets—'When I do count the clock that tells the time'—the 'c' is like a 'k', then the 't', then the 'c' again, then the 'ck', then 't', and then 't', making a perfect and evocative tick-tock.

In another one of Shakespeare's sonnets—'Devouring Time'—'devouring' needs a full and free series of movements of mouth and cheeks. If they are lifeless, then these syllables are flattened into one sound. If we feel the fine difference of sound

between 'd', a 'v' and an 'r', then we can feel
the climactic ring of 'g'. Then the 't' of 'time'
must come from a new attack. It is between
two consonants side by side, and there has to
be the tiniest pause—like a phantom breath.

Sea Bells

We travel on an Air France plane and hear the cabin attendant say 'fussyrseabells'. 'Sea Bells' can make us smile or think of them tolling for us as the plane plunges into the Atlantic. But in fact it would take just a few minutes of tuition to let pilots and cabin crews become comprehensible—and even avoid saying 'lyedeezanjentlmn'.

A light-hearted phrase from an eighteenth-century writer, Laurence Sterne, is at once an expression of the difference between English and French—'A dwarfish, little brisk fellow...' The order of words cannot be put into French—it is totally illogical. If spoken, the unexpected shifts from 'little' to 'dwarfish' and from both to 'brisk' must be savoured. There can be no correct reading—endless new patterns can appear if the unexpected is tasted at the moment of speaking.

To recognise the temptation to pinpoint and then fix with a closed definition is what makes so much acting so flat in both languages, often with texts of quality. This is where an actor must go far beyond technique and methods, and become sensitive to the tastes of letters as they constantly change place, relishing in the shifting detail and mini detail, the way the principal stress and the underlining are always on the move, at high speed. Then the actor is freed of rules and obeys a much more rigorous discipline, the recognition that what is right changes all the time as the feeling for the meaning is tasted.

There was a leading actor in Prague who came to England to flee the Nazi invasion. One of his famous roles was Othello, and he longed to play it in English. The Old Vic gave him the chance. Much of the time it didn't make sense, but it didn't matter as everyone knew the play. However, there was a moment of total incomprehension when he roared 'Dammaloodminkdamma'. Eventually we realised this meant 'Damn her, lewd minx, damn her'. Still he had power and a presence, a rare case where for a moment articulation didn't matter. Passion sweeps away all the rules.

When Laurence Olivier studied a new role, especially in Shakespeare, he would work for weeks on his face muscles. Taking the train from Brighton, where he lived, to rehearsals in London, he would, for nearly an hour, hold a copy of *The Times* in front of his face, giving the impression that he was reading the news. But in fact he was making his tongue, his lips and his cheeks shape themselves around the words he had memorised. Had he lowered the newspaper, his fellow passengers would have seen an extraordinary succession of grimaces. But Olivier knew that he was training his muscles so that the movements would become second nature and would shape every subtle intention as he played. He didn't need to speak slowly and carefully to articulate. It just seemed alive and true.

The greatest exponent in our time of spoken French was the fine performer Madeleine Renaud, wife of Jean-Louis Barrault. She could speak at lightning speed and still allow the unique individuality of each word to be felt and understood by the listener. Beckett wrote for her *Pas Moi—Not I*—which demands speed and dexterity in the fine quality of its detail. Madeleine succeeded in the amazing feat of speaking like a machine gun for tempo, but her tongue was so nimble, her thought so alive, that at high speed she could bring countless fine shades to the ever-changing flow of Beckett's thought. She was an amazing actor of pure virtuosity, only comparable to the way a violinist can play at lightning speed with a calm and a control in which no detail is lost.

A tempo in movement, music and speech is indefinable, like the current of life itself. It comes from the space that only relaxation can bring. When an acrobat is on a flying trapeze, his body, mind and feelings must be calm and free. Then, in the brief moment when he has released one bar and is in pure space, he can calmly reach out and catch the other. If there is any fear, any tension, if he reaches out a milli-instant too soon or too late, the fingers will miss the bar and he will fall. But if he is truly calm, he flies, and we fly with him.

Take My Word for It

A curious phenomenon arises when someone with a certain familiarity with both English and French pauses and in their own language says, 'How do you say...?' Very often it is almost the same word! It is as though the mind refuses this situation—it is so obvious that it can't be true. And this highlights a constant obstacle.

There are many words that are almost identical but which don't carry the same meaning. The basic substance is the same, except that the meaning can take on infinite overtones and undertones when spoken. There are countless examples, some comic, some the source of serious misunderstandings, but it is not the intention of this work to list them. They need to be discovered by trial and error.

One example springs to mind. 'I'm feeling out of sorts'—what origin, what image could have produced this odd but commonplace expression which the French call '*Je ne suis pas dans mon assiette*'? (I'm not in my plate.) What, when and how could this culinary expression have arisen?

'*Pourquoi?*' and 'Why?' may seem identical. The sense is exactly the same. But not the sound. '*Pourquoi?*' is an interrogation, the interrogator is pointing a finger at you asking for an explanation. 'Why?' is made of air—the 'y' sound at the end leaves the question open.

English today has a freedom from academic rules that makes it possible to use not only American slang but also street jargon. French also had this rich texture in the language that came out of the Middle Ages, in Rabelais and Villon, but the Age of Reason changed all this—the Académie Française arose to set unbreakable rules; and to this day, a highly prized elite meets weekly under the dome of their illustrious building to tighten the rules and to discuss what new words might be allowed to penetrate into the language.

'*Une femme blonde*' is one sound, one thought. When a noun comes before an adjective—the noun is what matters—the adjective is the decoration. In English, the order makes for suspense and surprise: 'A fair-haired . . .' *pause* . . . boy? girl? old lady? Or: 'A dreadful . . .' *pause* . . . A thousand possibilities are teasingly opened. Thunderstorm? A dreadful . . . argument? A dreadful . . . meal? It leads one on.

The essential definition of a word in French is that it is the *mot juste*—no more, no less than what carries the meaning on to its successor and is at its best at high speed. An English person speaking in French needs to practise speed without losing detail. Take a complete thought, a complex one, from the famous French poet Verlaine. '*Dans le vieux parc solitaire et glacé, / Deux formes ont tout à l'heure passé.'* One image—and the sentence is like one word.

For us, the *mot juste* is full of perils. There are countless examples, but one immediately comes to mind. 'Quite.' In England's English, this is a slightly disparaging 'not very'. But in American English, it's the opposite. I once auditioned an actor in New York and found him very interesting. I at once asked the producer of our show, who had also seen the actor many times, what he thought. The answer seemed tepid. 'He's quite good.' So I went on searching and found someone else, who proved very disappointing. Only later, much later, did I discover that for Americans 'quite' is a superlative. 'He's more than good,' the producer was telling me. But by that time it was too late—I had already replaced him. When the French say something is not bad, they use an astonishing adjective—*'pas terrible'*, implying that, in other words, the very worst was avoided.

In French, there is an everyday word identical in other languages—'*défendre*' (to defend). But in the French theatre, there is a special flavour given to this word. An actor offered a new part may say, '*Est-ce qu'il y a avec quoi me défendre?*' (Does it give me what I need to defend myself?), which suggests one aspect of the great unknown: what is an actor? Generally speaking, an actor does not want his or her inner self to be seen, so for centuries costumes, wigs, false noses, make-up were there to enable the secret self to defend itself against all prying eyes. '*Est-ce qu'il y a avec quoi me défendre?*' Today, this is beginning to give way, layer by layer, until in some pure and selfless moments the personality—even the person—of the player becomes transparent and a human truth is revealed.

I will just quote one very often-used word in French that is specially intriguing. '*Normalement*' ('normally'). This seems to express an anti-rationalist streak that the French would be pained to admit. '*Où est l'église?'* ('Where is the church?') *'Où est la gare?'* ('Where is the station?') or *'le café'* ('the café'). *'Normalement,'* comes the answer, *'vous descendez la rue, vous tournez à droite et normalement c'est sur votre gauche'* ('Normally, you go down the road, turn right and, normally, it is on your left'). A wondrous suggestion that we are living in an abnormal world, where during the night, it could have been spirited to the opposite side of the road. The common everyday use of *'normalement'* is as though we still carry in us memories of a pre-Cartesian world where the abnormal fell into place.

PART TWO

Dawn to Dusk

Dawn to Dusk

D.H. Lawrence used the words 'Mornings in Mexico' to capture the flavour of a daily experience, more vivid in Mexico than anywhere else. Each day begins with the beauty of sunrise, the hope of newness, of rebirth. Then as the day progresses, all the ancient pains, angers and pressures reappear: the guns are out, and the end of the day can easily be an explosion of violence or return to tiredness, disappointment, the hope of the dawn drowned in the greyness of the end of the day.

This cycle is present, often unseen, in every human activity.

One day in Paris, just after the opening of the Bouffes, a man came to see me with a strange tale. Like us, he too had been part of the euphoric happenings in 1968, along with a number of French actors with whom he had been working as director. The sharpness of the questioning of the meaning of cultural activities had left them all deeply shaken. Day and night, they sat together, trying to re-evaluate their lives and the meaning of their profession. When the dramatic period came to an end, order having been restored and most of France having set off for their summer holidays, his group was determined to maintain the fervour of the previous weeks, in which so much had been put in question. They all decided to move together to Geneva, to a deserted house on the banks of Lac Léman, where, as they toiled to make the place habitable, they continued with their discussions. What is theatre? What is a theatre group? How should one live one's life?

Night after night they wrestled with these vast issues. Gradually they became convinced that their first necessity was to have a performing space of their own. This led to another period of radical interrogation, which started with a rejection of all existing types of theatre building and ended with the conviction that for new work they should design and build something completely new. So they pooled ideas and resources: one sold his apartment, another borrowed money from his parents, and gradually they put together a very substantial sum of money. This enabled them to conceive boldly, so they drew plans for a collapsible and transportable dome that could adapt itself to every circumstance—from intimate plays to rock concerts. With their money, they bought tools and raw materials, and turned the outhouses and sheds of the Swiss villa into workshops.

At the outset, they were totally without manual skills, but, by sheer determination, they became highly proficient craftsmen, learning all the techniques they needed, from bending steel to joining wood to plastic. This took them over two years, but they never lost courage, and the human quality of their relationships grew steadily with each difficulty that they overcame. The day arrived when they were ready to mount the separate units, and on a camping ground outside a French provincial town they made a first trial. When they saw that the dome could come together as planned, they approached the authorities at one of the gates of Paris for permission to plant their construction on a piece of wasteland. They were now ready to give their first series of theatre performances. This was where they were now installed. When the director finished telling his epic tale, he invited me to go back with him to meet his group. I accepted readily.

It was late November, and when we reached that Paris suburb, night was falling with that particular greyness that makes one feel that snow cannot be far away. The dome was in position, but the skeleton was only partially covered by its plastic panes. Several young men and women on ladders were working at a feverish tempo, while inside the activity was at the same intoxicating pitch. I felt uncomfortable at not being able to help, especially as I was told that it was now a race against time to be finished before bad weather made work impossible. However, they made me feel welcome, and when, very late, the team agreed to take a break, I was invited to join them at supper in a small bistro nearby. It was a long table around which they pressed and squashed, their fatigue giving them new energy, so there was much noise, laughter and wine. I was impressed once again by the way hard work opens up personalities and cements a group. Here, I thought, leaving the building site, was a bunch of young people in love with theatre, who had truly found their own way and for whom the events of '68 had real meaning. When the meal was over and the hilarity died down, I asked many questions, which in turn prompted heroic and absorbing tales of their adventures.

'And now?' I asked.

'Now?'

'Yes, now,' I continued. 'What's your first production? What are you going to play?'

Even as I write, the reality of this story seems unreal, but in fact my question produced a strange silence. They all turned towards the director, who at once referred the question back to the team; their assurance was gone, the strength of purpose that was inseparable from their building work seemed no longer to have any place. One spoke hesitantly about shows for children, another about keeping the place active all day long. 'We have some ideas,' said a third. 'We are working on them,' said the director. I did not press the question, and the evening recovered its friendly glow. A few months later, by chance, I ran into the director. I hardly recognised him, for all his previous elation had gone. He told me that once the building was completed, the tension had dropped, the ties that had held the group so powerfully together had come undone, and he recognised that they were not able to transform themselves from the skilled artisans that they had become into actors with something to tell. They tried to put together a show, but they did not know that they had lost sight of their aim. The group splintered, scattered, the dome was abandoned, and the dream ended. With hindsight, the director realised that they had needed first to find out by trial and error, by playing to a public, anywhere, what theatre meant to them and what they wished to express. A long period of trying out every kind of improvised space, he now realised, had been necessary. Only then could they have begun to design a space which would be a natural and organic outcome of their work, which would correspond to their needs and which they could have filled. In putting the form before the content, their aim was undermined from the start. Here, I must stress that this is not aimed at the French—on the contrary, so many times in England I speak to architects building new theatres who would start from the shape and the geometry they liked, not starting from the living experience and the shapes that could serve this best. Which comes first: the cart or the horse?

This unhappy story has haunted me ever since. It showed acutely how often in any activity, however admirable the aim, something essential is missing, because the vision is incomplete, the cart has been put before the horse. It is the eternal problem of starting with a form, instead of a search for meaning. Only then can forms arise and find their place. How often have we seen this in the wheel of all revolutions—social, political, artistic, personal: a first sense of dawn, of spring that is cruelly followed by the jaws of what was fought against with so much heroic idealism gradually closing again. All forms are stepping stones to meaning. And meaning is the eternal grail that inspires the quest.

The Formless Hunch

It was a time when things happened, and even today I can't make out how or why. My conviction, that has lasted till today and is still with me, is that—although we must agonisingly examine all aspects of a decision and, if it's a bad decision, pull out whilst there is still time—in the end we don't make choices. The right choice makes itself.

A friend of mine asked a star football player what he felt when he scored the goal that won the match. He replied, 'Pure amazement. I don't know how it happened.'

I must now go far back into the past to find how I experienced the same moment of amazement that has guided me ever since.

Having been told by a flamboyant Italian film producer that no one would trust anyone under forty with the responsibility of being a director, I found myself, at the age of twenty-three, director of productions at Covent Garden, with no opera experience and with the exciting task of beginning with staging the most difficult of all operas, *Boris Godunov*. When I entered this august building, little did I realise that in the coming weeks I would live an initiation into mysteries that the following incident may help to reveal—the mystery of what I've called ever since 'the formless hunch'. I prepared, rehearsed, struggled to find my way in this new form. Then, suddenly, it was the first night. Here the process began with what was indeed a ritual—taking a bath, powdering oneself with talcum, carefully shaving the stubble off one's chin, and then putting on the clean white shirt, the cufflinks, the braces, bow tie and the uncomfortable coat called a dinner jacket, so as to vanish into the crowd of other similarly clad figures whose black shapes were necessary to bring out the splendour of the red plush and the shining gilt of the auditorium.

As I lay in my bath, I thought over the rehearsals, the complex scenic effects that my friend Georges Wakhevitch had devised, and above all the crowd scenes. This was my first experience of directing crowds—the hungry peasants of the first scene, the savage and ferocious movements of the revolution at the end—with of course not only stolid choristers not used to moving, but also soldiers from the nearest barracks happy to earn a pound or two, brought in for the occasion—and even a horse.

Most important was the second scene, the Coronation, when the leading character —the star, Boris—makes his first entrance, descending a red carpet covering a vast series of levels our designer had conceived to suggest the streets of Moscow leading into the Red Square, to be acclaimed by the people. I organised it like a military manoeuvre.

It took days to work out an intricate pattern—lines from one side criss-crossing with others from above, below and opposite, coming into place before the new Tsar began his descent. Somehow, it never seemed right. I came back to it day after day. Now I see that this agony was necessary.

Suddenly, when my mind was totally occupied with not cutting my chin with the razors of the time, it became crystal clear. My face still covered with foam, I rushed to the phone. 'Cliff!' I said to the stage manager. 'Quick! Go down to the dressing rooms, speak to each squad. Tell A not to follow B but to wait for D, while C must begin when they are halfway down, and B can then follow.'

A tiny moment of speechlessness, then a very loud 'You're out of your mind! They are all changing! The curtain goes up in an hour!'

I insisted. 'I'm sure. It'll work like clockwork.'

'I refuse,' he said. 'If one line is late, Boris will be blocked by the crowd. He won't be able to sing. The music will stop, the conductor will have a fit.'

All my work until then had been based on quietness, on gentle persuasive speech. But already in the opera world I had learnt that only dictatorial methods worked. Cliff was highly experienced, respected, twice my age. But I knew that the hierarchy gave me the answer. 'Do what I say!' I yelled and rang off. Drying my face, tying the tie again and again with shaking fingers before it became a neat black bow, I rushed out, grabbed a passing cab and was in my seat just as the curtain rose.

The first scene went well, then the great Kremlin bells chimed in the orchestra and the curtain rose again on Wakhevitch's giant staircase. With the first notes, the chorus began to enter, preparing for the star's entry. From one side the excited citizens, from another the solemn Boyars, then the lines of soldiers—a rich and complex tapestry of nearly one hundred moving figures unfolded. Unfortunately, the score was already deeply inscribed in my memory and as each bar passed, I could calculate how much time was left and how many lines of procession still had to appear. Never again have I known such a moment of terror. I wanted to cry out, 'Walk faster! You won't make it!' Worst of all, they were criss-crossing the very line that Boris had to follow to reach his podium of honour.

I became more and more convinced that Cliff, with his years of experience behind him, had seen clearly. They could not make it in time. I saw all the possibilities. A human traffic jam in the middle of the stage. A furious bass-baritone either elbowing his way ignominiously through his citizens to sing his noble assumption of the role of Tsar, or else out of his mind at the sabotage of his first London appearance, rushing furiously off the stage, followed by an incredulous set of agents pushing their way to his dressing room.

And then... as the last bars played, as though by magic, the last guardsman fell into place, Boris was already descending the royal stairway and, like a tide, the last crowd of choristers opened up. He stepped onto his crimson rostrum, and as the conductor's downbeat came, he intoned a rich first note. From then on, for me, a hunch seemed to make more sense than common sense.

I never believe in compliments and also never accept to take credit for the result. I know without a shadow of a doubt that this is the end product of long and arduous shared efforts by every member of the team. Only then is the ground prepared for the effortless action to appear. The clutter wiped away. A space is needed. An empty space.

When is a Space
Not a Space?

Not long ago, a distinguished critic wrote, after I brought a new production to London, 'When we came into the theatre, we saw an empty space. YAWN!' I always take critics seriously. It's surely time to take a new look at these two simple words—'empty' and 'space'.

At first, they seemed to apply to the place where we play, our playground. Tradition and long-standing habits had filled this with clutter, too much imagery, too many decorations, an excess of furniture and props. They clogged the imagination.

Emptiness was a starting point, not for its own sake, but to help to discover each time what was really essential to support the richness of the actor's words and presence.

Today, this battle has largely been won, although electronic shapes and sounds are now eager to rush in. But the clutter is more hidden. It's within the themes themselves—and within the actor. Anger, violence, hysteria, disgust and despair—these are so real that they must be expressed, powerfully, passionately. But light on a jet-black screen only reflects blackness. It's in the negative that an empty space has to be found.

Today, emptiness is an uncomfortable challenge to the director and the writer, as well as to the actor. Can a space be left open, beyond all one thinks, believes and wishes to assert? Every page of Beckett's plays is lightened with brackets enclosing the word '*Pause*'. Chekhov indicated the space in which the inexpressible could appear—with three dots . . . And Shakespeare surrounded every line with space. Theatre exists so that the unsaid can breathe and a quality of life can be sensed which gives a motive to the endless struggle.

The finest expression of emptiness is silence. There are rare moments in theatre when a deep feeling shared by actors and audience draws all into a living silence. This is the rare, the ultimate empty space.

o o o

John Osborne once said to me, 'An artist must always go against the tide.' I think this is an essential truth, but I'd like to make one addition: an artist must go both with and against the tide at the same moment. Not so easy. If in the theatre one isn't with the tide, one's out of touch, one isn't speaking the language of the moment.

Being with the mainstream isn't very difficult—the tide is powerful, and it is easy to let it sweep us along with it. But going against the tide is very difficult. First of all, one must recognise very exactly what the tide is and where it is going.

For instance, at a time when everyone has been numbed for so long by horrors, can one horrify? When every screen and so many street corners are drenched in blood, can tomato ketchup have any effect? Over sixty years ago, London audiences at *Titus Andronicus* fainted nightly and St John Ambulance was in attendance. A tiny torture scene by Jean-Paul Sartre made audiences scream. Once, even the word 'bloody' had its effect.

If we recognise that we've become numbed by shock tactics, that no scandal is scandalous, then we must face the fact that theatre, especially for its writers and directors, is suddenly losing its most reliable weapon. At a moment when social and political themes are what should— what must—concern us directly, how can we escape the banality of the obvious, the glibness of the outrage, the naivety of protest?

When the times are negative, there is only one current that secretly goes against the tide. The positive. The very vagueness of the word creates a negative reaction and shows how hard it is to detect. But unless its murmur is heard, not through platitudes, not through preachers' noble words, but through a reality that living theatre-people can bring, it has no function. We must enter the 'No' to find the 'Yes'. How?

If anyone proposes an answer, it's immediately suspect. But we must face the riddle.

In the theatre, we have rightly rejected cosy and degraded ideas of beauty, harmony, order, peace, joy. Now experimentally, directly, in our spaces, we need to rediscover what these hackneyed values once contained. A shock that awakes our indignation is cosy and is quickly forgotten. A shock that opens us to the unknown is something else and makes us feel stronger as we leave. The mainstream mustn't be despised, it has a great vocation. But to go against the tide, we have only one pathetic instrument, the human being. Finding the vital currents hidden in this misery is a formidable task.

○ ○ ○

When doing a play on conflict and violence, how often have I had to answer the same idiotic question: 'Do you think you can change the world?' Today, I would like to say, 'Yes, we can change the world.' But not in the old way that politicians, ideologists or militants try to make us believe. Their business is to tell lies. Theatre is, occasionally, capable of moments of truth.

If we are supremely ambitious and supremely modest, we see that an enormous amount is possible. There is a law of numbers. A tiny group in a tiny space can create something unforgettable. When there are more people, there is more vitality; there can be a vibrant energy. This world, limited in space and time, can be changed and sometimes so unforgettably that it can change an individual's life.

The tribes, the herds of human animals are made to work together. And yet, as my father told me when I was very young: If there were two people shipwrecked on a desert island and they made a parliament, one would be on the right and the other on the left.

In the tiny world of theatre, there are rivalries, hatreds, meannesses, fights ... but it is perfectly possible to go against the tide. Through a shared aim, shared needs, shared love of a shared result in theatre, from the creation of space ... the coming-together of an endlessly repeated climax of shared performance, again and again, something special can appear. Being together, working together, bringing a higgledy-piggledy assortment of haphazardly mixed spectators into a unity called 'an audience', makes it possible, for however short a time, for individuals who more than ever are each one in a confused, chaotic world of their own—these worlds can be changed. Every form of theatre has something in common with a visit to a doctor. On the way out, one must always feel better than on the way in.

PART THREE

Skyscraper

'Words, words, words.' We need them. There is no way out. They're never the end of something but a beginning, and every word we find in Shakespeare is a starting point.

The moment anyone says, 'Shakespeare thought', 'Shakespeare said', we are just reducing to an ordinary level the greatest mystery, the greatest enigma of all time in literature. We're trying to turn him into somebody telling us what we should think and feel about politics, religion, human beings on every level. But if we look more simply, we can see that there is no trace anywhere of Shakespeare's own point of view, except in his very special work, the Sonnets. Like in a diary, he expresses certain precise themes that are mainly related to his own personal experiences of love. This is the only exception. There are no characters in Shakespeare's plays where the author judges in advance: 'Huh, this is the bad guy', 'This is the monstrous woman', 'Here is a good person.' No. Each one, at the moment of speaking, expresses themselves with the full range of a human being. But like all human beings, some are shallow, some are turbulent. This complexity is the richness that the theatre shares with us. On stage we can meet the different levels of the person in a very short space of time, sometimes almost immediately. In everyday life this could take months or even years. In a soliloquy there is a concentration of what is lived through by a person, over days and days of feeling and thought. And this leads us straight to the 'skyscraper'.

A 'skyscraper' is a practical, available image, and at the same time it is related to the works of Shakespeare. In his Complete Works an infinite number of levels can be seen—theme after theme, character after character, line after line, and, in the end, word upon word. One can either rush past or feel that within there exist shifting levels of meaning. Some take you a few floors up, some pull you a few floors down. Sometimes they lead to that moment of astonishment, a silence when—as we say so easily—words fail.

From the top floor you have a view of the whole teeming world. You look down and see all the busy human beings below—the busy-ness of the marketplace. You know that it is as real as any other part of human activity. If you look carefully you may even see the police charging in and bashing people on the head. But at the same time if we look up we see the sky, the sun and the stars. They are always there.

Let's now look at two dreaded, dry and theoretical words, 'esoteric' and 'profane'. In all of Shakespeare, there is a natural movement that goes from the esoteric to the profane. Something is opened and then deliberately brought down into the soil of everyday life.

The most striking thing in the whole of Shakespeare's works is how he always returns back to earth. Throughout the themes in all his plays, through his characters, he raises us to a point where we recognise that we're together as an audience. There are moments in a play when we feel that we have all been touched at the same moment. We've come in as hundreds of heads, with hundreds of different preoccupations. We've come off the street—that busy state of chaos of the world—and now, in a short space of time, through the work of a little group of actors in a play, we're brought to a point where we sense a moment of truth. Something between two young lovers, something between Hamlet confronted by his own questioning and predicament. In so many ways we feel that what is being expressed is human. It means that at that very moment we don't know who is sitting next to us, and it no longer matters. We are what is called an audience, and 'audience' is a word in the singular. We have become one body. And that transformation always expresses itself in a fleeting moment of silence. You can feel it. The whirling of the different heads making noise that one can't hear. Then, suddenly, there's a moment when it all stops.

The only word that we know that really corresponds to this is that we're 'touched'. Every actor, every performer, knows that they and the audience become one, because everyone is *touched* by a moment of truth. There is, even briefly, a moment of suspension. A silence. Not an inert silence, not a graveyard silence, not a silence of old bones. But a silence that is full of life itself.

Shakespeare had the absolute need to make us feel once again that we're all part of the human race, all part of humanity. He does this by bringing us down to earth, without hesitation, with the crudest sexual jokes. A character in the play could easily have said, 'It's midday.' Not at all. 'The bawdy hand of the dial is now upon the prick of noon.' It's such a relief for everyone to have that natural laugh.

King Lear would never have had the same resonance if this extraordinary, powerful, multidimensional figure hadn't been balanced by something like a tiny skyscraper with many levels, but a child's skyscraper—the Fool. And the way the two of them interlink makes it possible for us to go from Lear's own tremendous journey to the Fool's common sense.

This is where the middle area of Shakespeare's work is so important, as long as one can see and welcome all of the crude, base humour. Today, there is such a fear, and rightly so, of anything too grand, too pretentious, and above all of anything that you could remotely call 'spiritual'.

Particularly in England. But, if you look at its tradition, especially its love of Nature, England is deeply mystical. However, this is almost always carefully concealed, and always covered with humour. Then, right at the bottom, you have an everyday level.

The great poet, Ted Hughes, told me that in Shakespeare's plays the word 'and' has a very special place. Sometimes, Hughes said, Shakespeare uses a word which for a large bulk of the audience might seem a bit too learned, but which would make the nobles and the intellectuals nod and say, 'Hmm, well said.' However, the rest of the audience—the common people, the thieves, the pickpockets, the whores—would say, 'What? What was that word?' Often in the same sentence, there would be an 'and', so that everyone can find the same meaning and come together.

Early in the middle of the twentieth century, actors were being told that they could never speak the words of our great national dramatist, unless they learned good King's and Queen's English and spoke like ladies and gentlemen. But suddenly there came actors who said, 'To hell with it; I'm going to play a prince with a North Country accent!' But this easily becomes an exaggeration, and today one sees that making the plays of Shakespeare 'contemporary' can easily lead to journalistic vulgarity.

Plays only exist in the present. A play is a renaissance. The plays written long ago are suddenly about us today. We experience just the quality of the moment. And here is a two-edged sword. It can either be the very stimulus to try going a few floors higher up the skyscraper without losing the sense that we are still rooted in the soil, or it can be the opposite: 'Oh, let's go two floors lower and make something contemporary.' It is so easy to fall into the trap of crudely importing television jokes, gags and nods to current events, which risks making us forget that there are higher levels. We're dragging down the plays and the characters where, instead, quality should always be present, rising and falling, in every situation, in every line, in every word. An actor takes out his mobile phone and suddenly discovers how easy it is to get a laugh if he says into his phone, 'To be or not to be?' But such things balance on a knife edge.

In this book, we constantly come back to my own working vocabulary. The most useful word is 'detail'. We say a line, and like all Shakespeare these lines are of such simplicity that they can be understood all over the world. 'To be or not to be.' I've often used this with actors as a working exercise. There is no limit to the different ways that this line can be said, and it colours every detail that follows.

Feel that there is more detail in the words, 'To be.' 'Be' is a simple, everyday word. Something can be felt within that simple 'To *be*.' There is detail and that detail colours 'or not to be'. Then the word 'question' takes on new detail. 'To be or not to be' brings us to the point where it's clear that there is something that can't be understood. Then the coming down to earth: 'That is the question.' Or the exact opposite. We have rushed past the fact that in the context of Hamlet's predicament 'To be or not to be' is about living or dying. 'That is the question' in this case is an opening to something more.

Each time we hear a soliloquy we're with an actor who is taking us on a completely new journey. If the actor is in a living interrogation—not of himself, nor of Shakespeare, but of that unknown character called Hamlet—then gradually we will be led to something which stops us in our tracks when he comes to 'Thinking too precisely on the event'. 'Thinking too precisely' at once links up with Romeo's 'Hang up philosophy!' Stop explaining, stop defining, stop trying to understand just with your rational powers. All that Descartes brought into European consciousness can go just so far. But there's a limit. At that point there is something which takes us again through the whole Works of Shakespeare, which is ' ... the name of *action*'. 'Action' brings us to a whole level of esoteric meaning, because it's there. What is the relation between thought and action? We have to act, but what is our part and in which play? We're here on this earth to act—we're not here just to sit, shut away as Hamlets: action goes a very long way. Detail in Hamlet's overall exploration takes us directly to many great traditions.

It takes us into Hinduism, to the heart of the Bhagavad Gita, when, before the great battle, Arjuna is being asked to take part in a massacre. He sees half of his family in front of him—his uncles and cousins. He is being asked to launch a war that he knows will kill all the people closest to him. Naturally, as a human being he stops—just like Hamlet. At that moment the semi-god Krishna tries to lead him, step by step, through many complex meanders. This directly relates to the same process in Hamlet, taking him to a point where he realises that he cannot abandon action. In the case of Hamlet we're right in the heart of unpretentious, simple but challenging esoteric thinking. Hamlet is asked to revenge his father without 'soiling' his mind. This is a call that we can never escape for the rest of our lives. If only all our generals, our leaders and the people who incite rebellion, mutiny, genocide, could ask themselves this question. Is it possible to go into what is understood to be 'rightful' revenge? His father has asked Hamlet for revenge. He can't fail to do his duty to his father who has been unjustly murdered. And yet he is told by this loving father to do it without soiling his mind. What does this mean? We would love for our leaders to occasionally ask themselves that question.

In Lear, Paul Scofield, one of the greatest actors I've ever known, never soiled his mind with theory or philosophy. Each time I started a discussion with him he'd stop me and say, 'No no, I have to play this.' And his way of acting a part was very simple. He was in his forties, he was playing King Lear, and, after preparing in the way he did, everything fell away and he just *was* the character. One can see it in the film. He's not impersonating, he's not, in actors' terms, *characterising* an old man. He hasn't studied 'How does an old man walk?' He really *becomes* a very special, complex, powerful, but very old man. He doesn't have to show it in the feeble way that many actors do by illustrating that he's in his dotage. He just is the unique person, King Lear, who is in full possession of everything but with a terror of going mad, of losing his brain. At the same time, the actor playing him is no longer the puppeteer controlling the acting. No: he *is* King Lear.

At every performance after Cordelia's death he would say the simple words (even simpler than 'To be or not to be'), 'Never, never, never, never, never.' Every single time, in the hundreds of performances we did, across the world, the rhythm of those five 'never's was never the same. The whole of what he, as a character, had been experiencing at that very moment was what gave the detail to the vibration, which went into the voicing of those particular words.

Shakespeare wrote at a tremendous speed. As a manager, he saw how urgently his theatre needed a new play. Everything suggests that many of his plays were written non-stop in one night. Which is the opposite of my dear friend, the much-admired Sam Beckett, who would spend a year dwelling on each phrase and trying to improve it, in deep humility saying, 'Yes but why? Why have I written that?'; 'What am I trying to say?'; or 'Why is this man standing, looking out of the window? Why isn't he sitting?' Beckett constantly suffered from writer's block: he would just stop at the end of a sentence that didn't seem to be right. Weeks, even months went by before he could start up again. With that marvellous reflection, though at the same time thinking so precisely, he was brought to a point that he could never go beyond, as only one person in history had done—Shakespeare.

The unique thing about Shakespeare is that he's unique. And that, perhaps uniquely in all writing, he had this capacity to be anywhere—in the street, as well as in the theatre, talking with the actors, at home and in the country. Above all in a pub, in the taverns, where so much of life went on. At the next table, he hears somebody telling news of court, at another table somebody talking about how hard it is to reconcile what you felt as a Catholic with what you're supposed to feel as a Protestant. He's absorbing all this. Second by second, all the impressions were being absorbed. But what most of us generally retain is a tiny number. So if you have this one unique human being, with a unique capacity to hear, watch, listen, and retain, there is no reason at all to exclaim, 'How could this country peasant know all that we people from the court, we people of learning, we people from university have spent so much time learning?' This is snobbish and repellent.

Shakespeare was born in the country with a love of nature, for the forests and the plants that we can see in so many of his plays. It is apparent that for all those who had said, 'Poor country yokel, what does this lower-class peasant know about higher things?' there was a boy who was absorbing everything around him. Today, one has no need to go to the countryside around

Stratford to receive the most wonderful impressions of the beauty of the earth, the plants, the flowers, the trees and the hills. It's quite obvious that with somebody as sensitive as this inborn poetic soul he never lost any of his impressions. That is the extraordinary thing about the human mind. We think that everything is forgotten. But deep down, every impression, second by second, is retained somewhere. And this strange, unknown quality of what we call 'genius'—in the same way as a musical genius—means that this whole universe of sounds can come without being called, just because they are needed.

Prospero in *The Tempest* recognises that within nature, before you get into the world of the cities and the courts, there is something that is called magic. Magic is used ruthlessly for power, both by Prospero as well as by those who want to murder him. Prospero's wish for revenge has tainted his mind, and he is hell-bent—literally *hell*-bent—on revenge. His deepest qualities emerge and make him recognise what is beyond revenge. So he breaks his wand and he drowns his book. He gives it all up to return to being a simple human being. At the very end of the play he asks for a prayer (again this isn't Shakespeare, it is Shakespeare through Prospero speaking of a prayer) that 'pierces ... mercy itself'. A prayer that is so sharp with clarity that it's like a needle, or a blade, that leads us to what may be the last word Shakespeare wrote—'free'.

And in 'free' are found all these aspects of the human outer and inner nature that completely cloud us from a sense of what a natural order could be. 'Freedom.' It can resonate in us in a way that brings together all the different levels of a unique 'something' called the Complete Works of Shakespeare. Works that contain all the esoteric teaching in the world. But not through a teacher preaching. Every moment is to be discovered and rediscovered, but not, however, by sitting at home and reading, because there again one would be betraying the real function of writing for performance. We should discover this every time the words and the characters are brought to life for us, and with us, in performance. Then, the structure of the skyscraper with all its levels can, for a moment, come into being. Its walls can melt away.

And the rest is silence.

The Mirror

The Mirror

Shakespeare said that Theatre holds a mirror up to nature. Of course this means human nature, human nature that can perceive the wind and the rain, and as the sonnet says, 'everything that grows'. There are many kinds of mirrors and Theatre can be every one of these.

Theatre can be no more than an old, dirty mirror, and this mirror can only show the sordid sides of human nature.

Theatre can be a dusty mirror, which blurs the image and covers up the wrinkles and blemishes, so as to give a soft and reassuring reflection of reality.

Theatre can be a shining but cracked mirror with spots of bright colour and blinding flashes through strident cries of protest and anger or bursts of stamping joy with explosions and energy which can only make more and more cracks and fragments and send us back into the world more angry than when we came in.

And of course, Theatre can also be the distorting funfair mirror which makes us laugh at our own deformities and those of others.

Are these the mirrors Shakespeare speaks of? Indeed, they all give glimpses of the human condition. But if we work in Theatre, we know we are called to strive towards what his Complete Works show—a mirror constantly cleaned and polished to reveal, layer by layer, what is hidden, what lies in darkness until for a brief moment light can penetrate and the mirror vanish. There is no longer the seer and the seen. We are touched deeply. The nature of human nature is astonishingly revealed.

161 244385 2

The Land Use Planning System

Two week
loan

Please return on or before the last
date stamped below.
Charges are made for late return.

WITHDRAWN

IS 239/0799